*C*hasing a

Nancy Kerrigan, a 24-year-old figure skater from the United States, looked radiant as she skated onto the ice at the Hamar Olympic Ampitheatre near Lillehammer, Norway. It was October 1993, and Nancy was competing at the Piruetten international skating competition. After two disappointing performances earlier in the year, she was there to show the world that her skating was back on track.

Her new long program, skated to music written by singer/songwriter Neil Diamond and performed by the Boston Pops orchestra, included six triple jumps. Nancy had been working hard on her routine, and it showed. She nailed five of the six triples perfectly.

But it was Nancy's artistic skill that was especially impressive. With elegant spins and graceful jumps, she moved like a ballerina on the ice. The judges awarded her six 5.9 scores in the artistic impression category, and that was enough to put Nancy over the top. She was the winner.

Nancy Kerrigan was back!

Just three months after that stunning victory, disaster struck. A frightening attack on Nancy before the 1994 national championships in Detroit injured her knee and threatened her Olympic hopes. But as she had many times before, Nancy battled back. **NANCY KERRIGAN: Heart of a Champion** tells her story, from the young skater with dreams of Olympic glory to the world-class athlete determined to make those dreams come true.

NANCY KERRIGAN
Heart of a Champion

by Mikki Morrissette

A Sports Illustrated For Kids Book

Bantam Books
Toronto • New York • London • Sydney • Auckland

Nancy Kerrigan: Heart of a Champion by Mikki Morrissette

A Bantam Book/March 1994

SPORTS ILLUSTRATED FOR KIDS and are registered trademarks of Time Inc. SPORTS ILLUSTRATED FOR KIDS BOOKS are published in cooperation with Bantam Doubleday Dell Publishing Group, Inc. under license from Time Inc.

Cover photo © Dave Black 1994

ISBN 0-553-48254-8

Published simultaneously in the United States and Canada

Bantam books are published by Bantam Books, a division of Bantam Doubleday Dell Publishing Group, Inc. Its trademark, consisting of the words "Bantam Books" and the portrayal of a rooster, is Registered in the U.S. Patent and Trademark Office and in other countries. Marca Registrada. Bantam Books, 1540 Broadway, New York, NY 10036

Printed in the United States of America

CWO   0 9   8   7   6   5   4   3   2   1

Contents

Rise of a Champion

1969   *October 13.* Nancy Ann born to Brenda and Dan Kerrigan in
        Woburn, Massachusetts.

1970   Nancy's mother is diagnosed with multiple neuritis, an eye
        condition that causes her to lose most of her sight.

1975   Six-year-old Nancy begins taking skating lessons in Stoneham,
        Massachusetts.

1987   Nancy performs well in the *New England Junior, Eastern
        Junior,* and *National Junior* tournaments.

1988   • *United States championships*   12th place
        18-year-old Nancy's first appearance in this
        important event.
        • *National Collegiate Championships*   first place

1989   • *United States championships*   fifth place
        • *World University Games*   third place
        • *U.S. Olympic Festival*   third place

1990   • *United States championships*   fourth place
        • *U.S. Olympic Festival*   first place
        • *Goodwill Games*   fifth place

1991   • *United States championships*   third place
        Nancy earns a place on the U.S. team that will compete at the
        world championships.
        • *World championships (Munich, Germany)*   third place
        In a surprising performance, Nancy wins the bronze medal
        behind U.S. teammates Kristi Yamaguchi and Tonya Harding.

1992   • *United States championships*   second place
        Nancy wins the silver medal and qualifies for the U.S. Winter
        Olympic team.

- *Winter Olympic Games (Albertville, France)*   third place
Nancy captures the bronze medal in her first Olympics.
- *World championships*   second place
- *March 8.* Officials in Nancy's hometown of Stoneham, Massachusetts, host "Nancy Kerrigan Day."

1993   • *United States championships*   first place
Nancy finally reaches the top, winning her first national championship.
- *World championships*
(Prague, Czech Republic)   fifth place
This disappointing performance leaves Nancy questioning her skills.
- *Piruetten international competition*
(Hamar, Norway)   first place
- *AT&T Pro-Am Challenge*   first place
Back-to-back victories show Nancy has returned to championship form.

1994   • *January 6.* Nancy is attacked before the United States nationals and withdraws from the competition. Her Olympic hopes are threatened. An investigation of the attack begins.
- *January 8.* Tonya Harding wins the nationals and Michelle Kwan finishes second. Nancy is later named to the Olympic team by the United States Figure Skating Association. Michelle is made an alternate.
- *January 17.* Nancy returns to the ice and begins training again for the Olympics.
- *February 23. Winter Olympic Games (Lillehammer, Norway).* The women's figure skating singles competition begins.

1 The Blow to a Dream

Nancy Kerrigan was feeling great. She glided gracefully around the skating rink at Cobo Arena in Detroit, Michigan, practicing her jumps and spins along with other skaters, as a few hundred people in the stands looked on.

It was Thursday, January 6, 1994, and the United States women's figure skating championships would begin the next day. Nancy, a 24-year-old from Stoneham, Massachusetts, was expected to win the national title for the second year in a row.

The Winter Olympics were just five weeks away, and the 1994 nationals would also serve as the tryouts for the United States Olympic Team. Only the top two finishers would make the team that would travel to Lillehammer, Norway, in February for the Olympic Games. Nancy had been skating so well that some experts predicted she would not only make the team but also win a gold medal at the Olympics!

One by one, the other skaters finished their workouts. Only Nancy was left on the ice. Finally, around 2:30 P.M., Nancy decided to call it a day. She started to walk toward the dressing room.

"Is that Nancy Kerrigan?" asked a man standing at the edge of the rink. The man was sweating and seemed nervous. He was taking pictures very fast with a camera. He pointed to Nancy as he asked the question. The person he asked, a coach of one of the other skaters, nodded, and the man with the camera left quickly. Later, other people would also recall seeing a man acting strangely.

As Nancy walked down the hallway to the dressing room, she paused briefly to talk to a reporter from the _Pittsburgh Post-Gazette_ newspaper. Suddenly, a man wearing a black leather jacket, a black hat, and light-colored pants raced toward the two people from behind. As he ran between them he swung a long metal stick and whacked Nancy hard just above her right knee. He kept running down the long corridor—past six startled witnesses—as Nancy collapsed immediately to the ground and began to scream with pain.

Nancy's three horrified cries could be heard throughout the nearly empty arena. While a small group of skaters, reporters, and family members quickly gathered around Nancy, a security guard chased after her attacker. But the man in the black leather jacket escaped by crashing headfirst through a locked plastic door and disappeared into the snow falling outside.

"It hurts so bad," sobbed Nancy. "Please help me."

Nancy's father, Dan Kerrigan, was one of the people at her side. He gently picked her up and carried her down the hallway into a private room. "It hurts, Dad," Nancy cried softly. "I'm so scared. Why me? Why now? Why?"

Police sergeant Karen Sousa interviewed Nancy soon after the attack. "She said she would never be able to recognize the guy," Sergeant Sousa reported later. "All she remembered is that all of a sudden somebody hit her. She definitely was in shock. She was crying."

Medical tests showed that Nancy's kneecap and quadriceps tendon were seriously bruised. (The kneecap is the plate of bone that protects the front of the knee. The quadriceps tendon is a strip of body tissue that holds the thigh muscle to the leg bone.)

Luckily for Nancy, no bones had been fractured. Had the blow been made an inch or two lower on her knee, Nancy's kneecap might have been shattered and her skating career likely would have been over.

The big question now was: Would Nancy be able to compete the next day in the nationals? One of Nancy's coaches, Evy Scotvold, said his skater is "really trying to be optimistic and stoic, but [at first] she was terrified. Nancy would like to compete, but how much pain is there? Can she stand it? Can she skate?"

The right leg is the most important one for Nancy, because she uses that side for takeoffs and landings in her jumps. Dr. Steven Plomaritis, who treated Nancy that day, was convinced the attacker had purposely aimed for the right leg. "He was clearly trying to debilitate her," he said. "The bruise may keep her from participating. Any time she lands on or bends her knee, that will put pressure on it when she skates."

Skating fans around the world wanted to know how Nancy was doing. That night she appeared on ABC television. "I don't want to lose faith in all people," she said. "It was one bad guy, and I'm sure there are others because this has happened in other sports. But not everybody's like that."

Nancy hoped to compete the next day as planned. But she knew that it might be impossible. "It's not the most important thing, skating," she said, trying to sound cheerful. "If I can't [compete], I'll have to deal with it. I'm okay. It could have been a lot worse."

After Nancy had limped back to her hotel, her father told a journalist from _The Boston Globe_, "Nancy is doing pretty well under the circumstances. It's me who's not doing well."

Nancy's coach wanted to do what was best for her.

"I want her to compete if she can," said Mr. Scotvold. "On the other hand, I want to protect her and make sure she doesn't do any further damage."

Around midnight, Nancy's agent, Jerry Solomon, told reporters that her knee was swelling up badly. "I'd imagine if it hasn't gone down by morning they're going to tell her she can't skate," he said. "She sustained quite a blow, not only physically but emotionally. She's really having to deal with both aspects of that. The only thing I can tell you is that she's pretty mentally tough. She doesn't like what's happened and she's a pretty strong fighter. You've got to factor that in somewhere."

By the next morning, Nancy could barely bend her right leg. The swelling had moved from the front to the back of her knee. Doctors drained two ounces of blood from the area.

Nancy couldn't even hop on her right leg. It would be impossible for her to compete. Nancy knew she would have to withdraw from the national championships. "I cried and cried," she said.

At a press conference to announce her withdrawal, Nancy said, "I'm pretty upset and angry that someone would do this, but I'm trying to keep my spirits up." Her voice broke a few times as the emotions of her announcement hit her. "I really wanted to skate today, but the doctors said I shouldn't, to prevent a worse injury."

Nancy and her family remained in Detroit to watch

the nationals. Two days after the attack, on Saturday night, Nancy was sitting in a private box above the ice at Joe Louis Arena, the site of the championships. Watching the final round of the women's competition with her were her parents, her 7-year-old cousin, and a few other people. Fans in the stands waved signs that read "We Love You Nancy."

An ABC-TV reporter asked Nancy how it felt to be watching the competition that night. "I'm pretty upset," Nancy replied. "I wish I could be out there. I feel I've never skated better than I have lately."

What probably upset Nancy more than missing the nationals was the thought that she had missed her chance to make the 1994 Olympic team. Nancy knew that if she had been able to compete, she almost surely would have finished first or second and earned a spot on the team. But now that a mysterious attacker had shattered that dream, would the U.S. Figure Skating Association (USFSA) give her a chance to compete in the Olympics anyway?

Nancy had competed in the Olympic Games in 1992. One of her teammates that year had been Todd Eldredge, a figure skater who hadn't been able to compete in the 1992 national championships because of back problems. Todd had been named to the Olympic team anyway because he had finished third in the world championships the previous year. USFSA rules state that skaters can be picked for the Olympics based on their medal-winning performance in either the nationals or the previous year's world championships.

Nancy, however, had finished a very disappointing fifth at the previous world championships. She wouldn't be given an Olympic spot based on *that* performance. So, there she sat, with a throbbing knee, watching skaters such as Tonya Harding and Nicole Bobek and Michelle Kwan and Elaine Zayak compete without her, and wondering if she had an Olympic future.

The skaters that night, perhaps a little ruffled by the attack on Nancy, generally did not have spectacular performances. Tonya, age 23, won her second national title with a strong program, featuring five triple jumps, but she didn't attempt her usual triple Axel move. Michelle, just 13 years old, finished second with an ambitious performance, but fell once on a triple Salchow and stepped out of a triple Lutz attempt. (See the glossary at the end of the book for descriptions of the jumps and other skating terms.)

Claire Ferguson, the USFSA president, had told reporters the day of the attack on Nancy that the rules were strict about requiring a skater to compete at the nationals in order to qualify for the Olympics. But, she added, "I don't think any doors should be closed. Our rules are stated pretty clearly, but it's a thick book and if you go chapter by chapter you can find something."

And indeed they did. Someone discovered rule 5.05,

which appears on page 193 of the rulebook, that said the Association's international committee was allowed to select skaters who had not been able to compete because of special circumstances. Late at night, after the nationals were over and Tonya and Michelle had earned their medals, members of the committee met to decide Nancy's fate.

"We're not so cutthroat as a sport that we don't recognize the right thing to do," said one member of the international committee, Carol Heiss Jenkins. Mrs. Jenkins coaches top-ranked skaters Lisa Ervin and Tonia Kwiatkowski, and was a gold medalist at the 1960 Olympics. "Even if one of my skaters was bumped because of Nancy, I'd vote for it," she said.

Other committee members agreed. It was decided that Nancy and Tonya would represent the United States at the 1994 Games. Michelle was named as an alternate to the team, which meant she would participate in the Olympics if either Tonya or Nancy could not.

Both Tonya and Michelle were pleased with their performances in the nationals, and said they were saddened that Nancy had been unable to compete with them.

"I came here to win and I did it," said Tonya. "It won't be a complete title without having competed against Nancy. At the Olympics it will feel complete, with Nancy there."

"It's a tragic thing," said Michelle's coach, Frank Carroll, about the attack on Nancy. "It'd be more tragic if Nancy wasn't given the opportunity to go to the Olympics. There's no question in my mind that if she'd competed she'd have finished in the top two."

After the nationals, Nancy returned to her parents' home in Massachusetts and began the difficult task of preparing her mind and body to be in top shape for the Olympic Games. It would take time, and careful rehabilitation, to get her knee back to normal.

Doctors told Nancy it would be two weeks or so before she could begin to practice the graceful jumps that she was noted for. But they were optimistic that her knee would be strong by February 6, the day the USFSA planned to evaluate her skating and see if she could, indeed, compete at Lillehammer.

The Olympic team was scheduled to fly to Norway on February 9. The women's figure skating championships would begin February 23. Would Nancy be ready?

"Nancy Kerrigan is not a victim," said Cindy Adams, a sports psychologist who works with Nancy. "She's a survivor. That's how we're going to look at this. She doesn't understand what's happened or why, but she's not going to let this get in the way of what she's set out to do."

Nancy was called a survivor because she had already overcome many obstacles to become a world-class figure skater. Coming back from this attack would probably be her toughest challenge yet. But Nancy was determined to keep pushing for her dream: to be the best figure skater in the world. It was something she had dreamed about since she was a young girl.

2 Brightness in the Dark

Nancy Ann Kerrigan was born October 13, 1969, in Woburn, Massachusetts. She was the third child—and the first daughter—born to Dan and Brenda Kerrigan. Nancy has two older brothers: Mark, who is five years older, and Michael, who is three years older.

The family lived in nearby Stoneham, which is a small town in eastern Massachusetts. It is about 10 miles outside of Boston, the largest city in the state. The Kerrigans still live in the same house they lived in when Nancy was born. It is more than 100 years old!

Nancy's father supported the family by working as a welder. He also worked for a time in a General Foods plant. Her mother took care of the home and Nancy and her brothers.

Life for the Kerrigans was normal enough, until one

spring day in 1970, when something happened that changed all of their lives. On that day, Nancy's mother was driving near their home, with her three children in the car. Nancy was just 7 months old.

Mrs. Kerrigan had some sort of a virus, but she hadn't gone to see a doctor. Suddenly, as she was driving, her vision blurred. Medical tests showed that she had developed a condition called multiple neuritis [new-RYE-tis]. It affects the nerves in the eyes. Had the virus been treated earlier, there probably would not have been permanent damage. Instead, the nerves in Mrs. Kerrigan's eyes were harmed and could not be repaired.

Gradually, Mrs. Kerrigan lost her sight. Before long, she could not see at all with her left eye. Today, she is able to see only out of the inside corner of her right eye. She sees only shadows and some colors, and she can tell the difference between light and dark. She is considered to be blind.

"If you were in my house and sitting at my kitchen table talking with me, you'd think I knew you," she once told a reporter from *Sports Illustrated For Kids* magazine. "But the next day, if I saw you in my driveway, I wouldn't know who you were. I can't see faces."

Mrs. Kerrigan's blindness posed a challenge for family members when the kids were growing up. If someone needed to leave a message for her, they would write a note in large block letters so it would be easier to read.

Most kids have to be reminded to keep their rooms picked up, but because Mrs. Kerrigan could not see, that request had a special meaning in the Kerrigan household. "You didn't leave anything on the floor because you didn't want her to trip over it," said the oldest son, Mark. "But you could get away with a few things, too, like a dirty face or dirty hands at the dinner table. But if I wore a baseball cap at dinner, you'd hear, 'Take that hat off.' "

When the kids were young, Mr. Kerrigan had to do all the driving. He also did most of the shopping, the cooking, and the laundry.

But Mrs. Kerrigan wasn't about to let her loss of sight keep her from leading an active life. She enjoyed sports and went snow skiing for the first time after she had lost her sight. She still loves the sport. Usually she follows close behind another skier who shouts out to her whether to turn right or left while gliding down a hill.

She also took up waterskiing for a while, until the day she moved wide of the boat that was towing her and ended up in the path of another boat. "The scare of a lifetime," she recalls. And a few years ago, Nancy taught her how to in-line skate. "Come on, Ma, you can do this," her daughter encouraged her.

Mrs. Kerrigan was also not about to let her problem

keep her from enjoying her children and encouraging them to be active, too.

Nancy grew up as part of a very close family. That included not only her parents, but loads of aunts and uncles and cousins who lived in the same area. Her grandparents—her mother's parents—lived two houses away, and often prepared Sunday breakfast for the whole family.

As a reporter for _The Boston Globe_ wrote in 1992, "Friends and relatives are constantly coming and going. No one ever knows how many people will show up for dinner."

When they were kids, the entire family—even mom— would skate on a nearby pond together in the winter. They would join several other families at a lake in the summer.

"My kids always played a lot of games together," says Mrs. Kerrigan. "As a family, we would go skiing in New Hampshire, or snowmobiling. We're the type of family that even spends New Year's Eve together. We'd go to the same parties our kids went to."

Nancy enjoyed being surrounded by her family and friends. "Thank goodness my parents made sure I kept things in perspective and had a pretty normal life," Nancy said, as she talked about her hectic life as a famous skater. "My family is real close. Not just my parents and my brothers, but my grandparents and cousins, too."

As a kid, Nancy seemed like she would be the Kerrigan who would go out into the world to make a name for herself. She was very daring as a child. Because the family's house was so old, it had creaky, scary places. For 5-year-old Nancy, the dark cellar, where the family washing machine sat, was the *spookiest* place. She would never go down there alone.

But that is the only thing her mother remembers Nancy being afraid of as a kid.

There were some things *adults* were afraid of for her, but young Nancy seemed to have no fear herself. Sometimes she would get up onto the six-inch-wide boards that edged around the deck outside her parents' house and pretend she was walking across a balance beam. Her Uncle Scott usually got very nervous about it, worrying that she would fall. "Of course I won't fall," Nancy would reply. "I have all the balance in the world."

Other times, little Nancy would carefully crawl up the inside of a doorway until she was hanging by her fingertips from the top edge. She would wiggle her body and kick her legs around while making monkey noises. "Wooh, wooh, wooh," she would grunt.

Nancy's favorite companion, in fact, was a monkey. It was a stuffed animal she called Melvin. Starting when she was about 3, she took Melvin nearly everywhere. If she stayed overnight at her grandmother's, or at a girlfriend's house, Melvin went with her. Even as an adult, after Nancy rented her own house near a practice rink in Cape Cod, she moved faithful, old Melvin with her.

Nancy has always been kind to people, a trait she had as a young child as well. It is that quality of hers that Nancy's mother is most proud of even today. "I have people say to me all the time, 'You must be so proud,' " Mrs. Kerrigan says. "I have a hard time with that question because I know they are referring to how well she skates. But I am constantly proud of Nancy because in all honesty she is truly a kind person, she's caring. I'm not saying this to be a mother that's bragging, I'm really not. I really feel this way. Ninety-eight percent of the time, Nancy is thoughtful and caring. And that matters the most to me, because skating is not the person."

Once, when she was 6 years old, Nancy went skiing with a group of family and friends. It was the first time most of the people, including Nancy, had ever gone skiing. As Nancy was going up the hill on a T-bar, a simple device that lifts skiers up the mountain, she noticed one of her mother's girlfriends had slipped and fallen. "Oh stay there," she yelled down to the woman. "I'll be right back. I'll come help you get back up."

Nancy showed her natural kindness in other ways, as well. During all the years before Nancy was old enough to drive herself to skating practice, she relied on a number of adults to get her to and from the rink everyday. One of the drivers, whose son skated with her, will never forget that Nancy didn't take anything for granted. As he gratefully told her parents several years later, "Day after day, week after week, year after year, Nancy never got out of the car without saying thank you."

Another family friend says her favorite memory of Nancy as a kid was that she always kissed everyone good night before going to bed, even visitors. Nancy was the only child she knew who did that. "And that was so nice," the family friend recalled. "That used to make me feel so good. Usually the little kids would all just disappear and go to bed. Nancy always had to go and give everybody a kiss good night."

Nancy wasn't perfect, of course. She was a normal kid who refused to eat green beans, loved to chow down on candy, and pestered her parents about getting a dog. Some nights it was hard to get her to bed as early as her parents thought she should.

There were also the normal everyday squabbles among the Kerrigan kids. When they were young, one of Nancy's brothers nicknamed her "Ug," which is short for "ugly." Nancy wasn't too impressed when her brother carved the nickname and her birthdate into a fresh batch of cement near the house: "UG—October 13, 1969."

Nancy used to drive her brothers nuts when they watched television together. Nancy tended to cry at sad shows, laugh loudly at comedies, and scream at scary movies. But what made her brothers go ballistic was when she actually *talked* to the television. "Let the rest of us watch this," they would yell. "Do you have to keep talking?"

But Nancy usually did things the right way, according to her mother, because she was always "a people pleaser. If you want people to like you, you tend to do things the right way, I guess."

Nancy was also very careful about the way she looked. "Even when she was little," Mrs. Kerrigan says with a laugh, "she always asked, 'Does this look okay? Are you sure this is okay? Does this go with this?' "

And Nancy was a born performer. When she was a preschooler, the family would be seated at the dinner table, music would be playing, and sometimes Nancy would decide to entertain everyone by dancing around.

"She wanted to be the whole show," Mrs. Kerrigan recalls with a smile. "And my father would be here saying, 'Head up, head up, keep your head up,' and Nancy would be dancing to the music, and the more people that watched her the more she liked it."

Along with her kind nature, Nancy already had many of the qualities that make a world-class athlete: confidence, athletic ability, a love of performing in front of others, and a supportive family. All she needed was to find the right sport. That would happen very soon.

3 Rise and Shine

Nancy started figure skating once a week when she was 6 years old. She took lessons at the Stoneham Arena in Stoneham, where at first she was just one of about 200 kids whose parents paid $30 for 10 lessons.

As Nancy said recently, "I had no style when I was a young skater. When I was little, I was a spaz. All I could do was go back and forth and up and down the ice real fast." But after working at her skating for a while, Nancy began to show talent for the sport, and started to win small local competitions.

The coach who taught the kids' class suggested to Nancy's parents that Nancy take private lessons to develop her skating skills further. Mr. and Mrs. Kerrigan talked it over with Nancy, who was interested in finding out how good a figure skater she could be.

"We went along with it," recalls Nancy's father. "And we went one step at a time. Every year she had a little goal. And every year she went a little further."

"She never stood still," Mrs. Kerrigan adds. "She never went backwards. Not ever. She always went ahead, always doing better than the year before. "

It didn't surprise anyone in the Kerrigan household that Nancy was turning out to be a gifted athlete. As a child, Nancy preferred sports to toys. She didn't spend much time with dolls or coloring books because she wanted to keep moving, to keep active.

"She was into anything that was physical, anything you could *do*," Mrs. Kerrigan remembers. "She was not somebody who would sit down and play quiet."

Nancy enjoyed riding her bicycle around the neighborhood. One of her favorite activities was swimming in the pool in the backyard. She also loved to go diving at a nearby pool, often getting tips from her grandfather. For a while, Nancy was convinced that she would be a good diver.

"I'd be good at this," Nancy would tell her parents. "Look at my shoulders. I have big shoulders."

Sometimes she'd think about becoming a gymnast. "When I finish skating, can I take gymnastics?" she would ask.

"Sure, I think you'd be good at that," her mother would reply. "When you want to stop skating, you can take gymnastics, but you've got to stop skating first."

Of course, Nancy never stopped skating, so she never became a gymnast.

By the time Nancy was 8, she was skating every chance she could get. By the fourth grade, she was so in love with the sport that she was willing to sacrifice nearly everything for it.

Nancy was not an A student at school—mostly B's and an occasional C—but she stayed out of trouble. She knew that if she got into trouble and had to stay after school, she would miss afternoon practice at the rink. She *never* wanted to miss a skating session.

"People thought she was crazy," Mrs. Kerrigan recalled to *Sports Illustrated For Kids*. "She'd get up at 4:30 in the morning to go to a rink. 'Are you nuts? What do you want to do that for?' people would say. But that's what she did. She didn't question it."

Every once in a while Mrs. Kerrigan would wake her daughter up and hear the groggy girl say, "I don't think I want to go today." Mrs. Kerrigan would reply, "Okay, fine, see you. I'm going back to bed."

Ten minutes later, Nancy would be out of bed and in her mother's room saying, "Oh, I have to go." Mrs. Kerrigan would respond, "No, you don't have to go. Of course, you don't *have* to go."

But Nancy was determined. "I know I don't have to go," she would say, "but I want to."

Sometimes even Mrs. Kerrigan thought her daughter was crazy, but she got up to make her breakfast anyway. "I never could make much sense of it, getting out of your bed at 4:30 to go to a rink," she says now, obviously proud of the dedication her daughter showed to her chosen sport.

Since Nancy's mother cannot drive, her father was the one who got Nancy to practice every morning before she was old enough to drive herself.

"Nancy and I would get up, then I'd wake Dan up," Mrs. Kerrigan remembers. "I'd make Nancy's breakfast. What's the big deal about a glass of juice and a bowl of cereal? Dan would drive her to the rink, get on the Zamboni [machine] to make the ice, take a nap while she practiced, drive her to school, and then go to work himself."

It turned out that Nancy's first coach was right about Nancy's talent. But in figure skating, as in all sports, there are no guarantees that hard work will bring success, fame, and fortune. The Kerrigans had no way of knowing that their young daughter would someday be competing at national championships, world championships, and the Olympics; or making thousands of dollars by performing at ice shows or in television commercials.

Yet they woke up with her every morning. They traveled with her when she started competing in, and winning, local competitions. Then it was regional tournaments, and then national competitions. "Since Nancy started skating," says Mr. Kerrigan, "the family hasn't been on a real vacation. We go to skating events."

Because Mrs. Kerrigan cannot see very well, Nancy has found ways to help her mother follow along when she has a new skating routine: She acts it out for her parents. "I do it out on the floor in the living room," Nancy says. "I use my arm movements, everything, so my mother can see it."

During live performances at a rink, of course, it's never been that easy for Mrs. Kerrigan to follow along, even if she knows the program. "I can't tell one jump from another," she says. "If I watch her arms I can't tell what her legs are doing." Mrs. Kerrigan watches tapes of Nancy's routines over and over at home later.

For the Kerrigan family, the hardest part of supporting Nancy in her skating career was finding the money to help Nancy get the coaching she needed. As Nancy improved, her skating lessons became even more expensive. As with most world-class figure skaters, the cost of Nancy's training eventually soared to $50,000 annually, which is more than Mr. Kerrigan's salary paid him.

"We are really, truly so average when it comes to the house, the way we live, the money we have," says Mrs. Kerrigan.

So how did they do it? Mr. Kerrigan worked one full-time job, and two more jobs on the side. He took out tens of thousands of dollars in loans from a bank. "But there was never any question, never any pressure on Nancy," he says. "We always told her that if she wanted to quit, she could quit."

Nancy's brothers sometimes felt a little jealous of all the attention Nancy was getting from their parents. But most of the time, they understood. Skating was what Nancy really wanted to do, and she was entitled to the full support of the family.

"This is not to sound conceited, but you really have to be a certain kind of parent to do this," Mrs. Kerrigan says. "It's not just the money. It's getting up at 4:30 every day. But we just did it. I don't know why. It never made any sense. We just did it."

Even though the time and money her parents have put into her skating career is paying off, Nancy will never forget the sacrifices her family has made on her behalf. Perhaps that is one major reason Nancy feels apologetic.

"It made me feel guilty," Nancy once admitted to a reporter. "I feel like everything they did was for me. It's scary when they are spending so much money and you don't know what you will get for it."

Driven by her dream of becoming a champion, though, Nancy skated on.

4 Shaping a Champion

Nancy's teenage years weren't like those of most girls. As she had been doing since she was 8 years old, she got up in the dark every morning for early skating practice. Then, she went to classes at Stoneham High School.

After school, she returned to the rink for more training. Then she had dinner, did her homework, and went to bed at 7 P.M. so she could start it all over again the next morning. There was usually no time left to hang out with friends, go to a mall, or check out the latest movies.

"I lost a lot of friends when I started skating because I just wasn't around," Nancy admits. "And some of them thought I was getting special treatment because I would arrive at school late and leave early. But I really didn't care what they thought. I just wanted to skate. It was an irresistible challenge."

After her senior year of high school in 1987, Nancy competed in the New England Junior tournament, where she finished third. (There are different levels of competition in figure skating, based upon the skaters' ability. Skaters must pass a test to get from one level to the next. Senior is the highest level, and junior is a step below that.)

That third-place finish enabled Nancy to compete in the Eastern Junior championships, where she finished second. That placing gave her a spot at the National Junior tournament, against the best young skaters in the country. Nancy made a strong showing in her first national competition, and finished fourth.

Those performances moved Nancy up into the elite world of figure skating, where the competition gets tougher, the training more strenuous, the coaching more intense, and the expenses higher and higher. It seemed that there was no stopping Nancy, or the ever-increasing cost of figure skating.

"It grew and grew," recalls Mrs. Kerrigan. "And every time it grew bigger, I got headaches and stomach aches and said, 'Oh God, no.'"

Nancy had graduated from high school in spring 1987, and started to work part-time as a waitress at a

Friendly's restaurant and as a salesclerk at a store called Frugal Fannies. She did that to earn spending money.

Nancy's parents couldn't give her an allowance because they were spending so much money on her skating. One expert says that a figure skater who is training to become a world-class competitor spends anywhere from $20,000 to $100,000 every year!

This is how the dollars add up:

- An experienced choreographer, who helps the skater plan his or her movements and how these will fit into the music they chose, costs $5,000 to $10,000.
- Good coaching costs at least $50 an hour.
- Some of the most expensive costumes, such as the specially-designed outfits Nancy wears in competition, cost about $5,000 each.
- Quality music recordings for the performances are about $2,000.
- Private rink time costs between $100 and $250 an hour.

Living expenses, skating equipment, physical therapy, health club membership, weight training, sessions with a sports psychologist to deal with the mental side of top-level competition, and travel costs for the skater, family, coach, and choreographer are all additional expenses. In some cases, the families of talented skaters move to one of the dozen or so places, such as Colorado Springs, Colorado, or Lakewood, Ohio, where top coaches work. Other families pay for their children to live with a coach or another family in one of these skating capitals.

The U.S. Figure Skating Association and private sponsors sometimes help Olympic hopefuls pay part of the cost of their training—but not much of it.

Though most of the financial burden for a skater's career falls on his or her family, only the skater is responsible for seeing that the investment pays off. Most skaters who dream of competing in the Olympics must spend four hours a day, six days a week, on the ice. They must do weight training a few times a week to strengthen their bodies. And most of them take ballet or jazz classes to improve their rhythm and grace on the ice.

The competitive skating season runs from the fall through the spring. But there is no such thing as a summer vacation. Carlo Fassi, who coached former Olympic star Peggy Fleming in the 1960's, says, "If you stop for two or three weeks, it's grueling to get into shape again."

There are hundreds of girls who want to become skating stars. "It's very often the vision of Dorothy Hamill," says skating coach Don Laws of the young woman from the United States who won the gold medal at the Winter Olympics held in Innsbruck, Austria. "Her Olympic year was 1976, but they still idolize her. All the young ones see themselves going to the Olympics."

To stay ahead of the pack, skaters who want to be the next Dorothy Hamill (or Kristi Yamaguchi, an American who won the gold medal in 1992) must deal with many temptations and distractions. A social life is only one thing to go out the window. Top-quality skaters must also make sure to keep their weight down. That's not always easy, especially for growing girls, even with a tough workout schedule.

Skaters simply have to shut out anything that will interfere with their tough practice schedules. Nancy has always had enough determination to do that.

Her constant schedule of training, traveling, and competing usually takes time away from everything else. For example, her engagement to an accountant named Bill Chase, after the 1992 Olympics, was called off, partly because they simply didn't have enough time to be together. And she had to quit taking business classes at a local college, where she enrolled in 1988, because her skating schedule was too tight.

Nancy finally did finish a two-year associate of arts program at Emmanuel College in Boston in 1992, and tells young people that getting an education is important. "School is so important," ⬤ says. "Skating isn't everything. I see kids so absorbed in it. Your body can't last forever, but your mind does. So you need an education."

Competition by competition, Nancy's dedication began to pay off. She entered her first United States national championship in 1988, and finished 12th. Later that year, she finished first in the National Collegiate Championships. She followed that up with four consecutive first-place performances at minor competitions.

At the 1989 nationals, Nancy leaped from her 12th-place standing of the previous year to fifth. Bronze medal performances at the World University Games and the U.S. Olympic Festival were two more highlights of that banner year. (The World University Games is an international competition among student-athletes. The Olympic Festival is a competition among United States Olympians and Olympic hopefuls.)

Sometimes Nancy was very happy with her performance. Sometimes, even if she finished high in the standings, she was disappointed. She wanted to be perfect.

At the 1990 nationals, Nancy missed qualifying for the world championships by only four-tenths of a point! She finished fourth, just behind Holly Cook, from Utah, who went on that year to finish third in the world championships.

Figure skating competitions, at that time, were made up of three parts: the short program, the long program, and the compulsory figures. Nancy had scored better than Holly in both the short program and the long program at the 1990 nationals, but not in the compulsories.

During the short program, which must be less than 2 minutes 40 seconds long, the skater does eight required moves: three jumps, three spins, and two footwork moves. The long program lasts for 4 minutes and allows the skaters to create their own routines. At that time, the short program counted for 20 percent and the long program counted for 50 percent of the skater's total score. The compulsory figures, in which skaters trace specific patterns on the ice, was worth the other 30 percent of the scoring.

(Compulsory figures are no longer included in singles competition. Today, the short program makes up one-third of the skater's score, and the long program makes up two-thirds of the score.)

Nancy, her family, and her hundreds of fans had a hard time understanding how Nancy could have been edged out of a place on the U.S. team. "How can you beat somebody on seventy percent of the marks and still not get to go?" Mrs. Kerrigan recalls the family wondering. "I don't understand the marking system anyway, so I never could understand it."

Skating does have a complicated scoring system. Skaters usually perform before a panel of nine judges. Each judge gives each skater two marks: one for technical merit and one for artistic merit. The technical merit mark tells how well each skater performed his or her moves. The artistic merit mark is for style, grace, ease of movement, and how well the skater interpreted the music. Judges score a skater from 0 points to 6 points, with 6 being perfect.

The judges' scores are not added together to figure out who won. Instead, each judge's scores are used to rank how the judge thought that skater's performance compared to those of other skaters.

Mrs. Kerrigan remembers asking Nancy at the time why she wanted to keep working at a sport that had such a strange method of judging its athletes. "Why are you killing yourself in this sport?" she asked. "Why don't you quit?" But Nancy wasn't ready to quit, no matter how upset she was.

It didn't take long after the disappointment of the 1990 national tournament for Nancy to bounce back. But first she had to skate her way through a conflict between doing what she thought would please her mother and doing what her coaches thought would please the judges and help her career.

That summer Nancy was invited to skate in the Olympic Festival. Nancy's coaches, then and now, are

Evy and Mary Scotvold, a husband-and-wife coaching team who also worked with 1992 Olympic silver medalist Paul Wylie.

Mary Scotvold is Nancy's choreographer, and one of Mrs. Scotvold's jobs is to help select the music and the movement and the look of Nancy's program. While looking through a magazine, Mrs. Scotvold was excited to see a picture of a long-sleeved, gold-beaded, open-backed white dress. She knew it would be perfect as a skating costume for Nancy, whose elegant looks and dark hair would look wonderful with the white dress. Add white earrings, white hair ribbons, and white skates, Mrs. Scotvold knew, and Nancy would be a vision of beauty. Mrs. Scotvold sent the design to a dressmaker.

But Mrs. Scotvold didn't realize that Nancy's mother would not be able to see Nancy wearing a white outfit against the white ice because of her vision problem.

The outfit was finished a few weeks before Nancy skated in the 1990 Olympic Festival in Minneapolis. She showed the costume to Nancy, whose immediate reply was, "I can't wear that! My mother can't see it."

But by then it was too late to find a different outfit. Wearing the skating dress, Nancy was all but invisible to her mother. "If she stood right there," Mrs. Kerrigan said later, pointing right in front of her, "I could see it. And it looked beautiful, regal."

Nancy was disappointed that her mother wouldn't

be able to see her, but she pulled herself together and skated a wonderful performance. She finished in first place in the competition!

A few weeks later, U.S. Figure Skating Association officials called Nancy to say that Holly Cook had withdrawn from the upcoming Goodwill Games, an international competition to be held in Seattle, Washington. Countries around the world would be sending their top skaters to compete. The Goodwill Games organizers would pay her $5,000 to skate in the tournament. Would Nancy be available to help represent the United States?

Nancy didn't have to think twice. The Goodwill Games were only two weeks away, but she said she would be ready.

Before she knew it, Nancy was competing for the first time against some of the world's best skaters. As she entered the final round of the championships, she was in second place, right behind world champion Jill Trenary. If she finished in the top three, she would be known in skating circles around the world. She would be considered a medal contender for the upcoming Olympics. After working at her sport for so many years, she was on the verge of becoming a star!

That kind of pressure, however, proved to be too much for Nancy. She fell three times on triple jumps during her performance, and ended up finishing in fifth place. She left the ice in tears.

"Nerves took over," Nancy said later. "I became so negative that I thought I stunk if I missed one jump." That loss of self-confidence during competition was a problem Nancy would face again and again for several more years.

"What happened in the Goodwill Games was traumatic," said Mrs. Scotvold. "A lot of people think Nancy is more experienced than she really is. But . . . she was probably not ready for the position she was in at the Goodwill Games. She wanted to beat Jill [Trenary] and Kristi [Yamaguchi, who was also competing] instead of focusing on what she does. Sometimes skaters get carried away with trying to outdo one another instead of concentrating on their own program."

But, again, Nancy did not want to quit trying. As Mrs. Scotvold said at the time, "It's all about coming back. You can fall and it's not even your fault sometimes because you catch an edge. Some skaters give up. We're on her about that all the time."

Nancy realized that to help combat her fears, she had to remember that "I've done these things a million times in practice."

"I'm proud to know," Mrs. Kerrigan says, "that through all of the bad times she was willing to stick with it. She didn't let it get her down. Maybe she felt bad for a while too, but she had something within her to keep trying."

5 Taking on the World

Nancy had performed well in almost every figure skating competition she had entered since she was a kid. Her best performance ever in a major event was her fourth-place finish at the 1990 United States championships, and that certainly was something to be proud of. But she had yet to finish in the top three at a national championship and earn a spot on the U.S. figure skating team. In 1991, she hoped to change that.

At the time, Nancy was one of five women considered to be the very best in the United States. The others were:

- Jill Trenary, a 22-year-old from Minnesota, who was the three-time national champion and defending world champion.
- Kristi Yamaguchi, a 19-year-old from California,

who had been the runner-up to Jill two years in a row at the nationals.

- Tonya Harding, a 20-year-old from Oregon, who had been in second place at the previous year's nationals before a nasty case of the flu—which left her skating with a temperature of 103 degrees—bumped her out of the running.
- Holly Cook, 21, who had barely edged Nancy out of a medal the previous year.

All five skaters were pointed toward a showdown at the 1991 U.S. championships to be held in Minnesota that February. Jill would have been the favorite, because she was the defending champion and she would have been competing in front of her home-state crowd. But Jill was recovering from ankle surgery and could not compete. Her absence left the championship up for grabs!

Kristi, whom many experts figured to capture the championship in Jill's absence, led 13 other skaters after the short (or "original") program, which is the first of the two rounds of competition. (The compulsory figures competition had been eliminated by 1991.) Tonya was in second place, Nancy was in third, and Holly was in fourth.

Before the final round of competition, the long (or "freestyle") program, Nancy felt confident. To deal with her problem of getting too nervous in competitions, she had been learning ways to calm herself down and keep her confidence up. She also knew that her parents were in the audience, which always helped her to feel secure. "My mother can't see with the clarity you and I have," she told a reporter, "but she's such an inspiration for me to skate well."

Mrs. Kerrigan would be following her daughter's performance on a television monitor. When she tried to watch Nancy from the stands, all she saw was a blur.

Even with the television, Nancy's mother has to press her nose right up against the screen to see anything. "I can tell if Nancy falls," Mrs. Kerrigan once told a reporter about watching on the TV monitor. "I can tell if she does a spin. The television has made it possible for me to see one hundred percent more than I would in the stands, but not the way you do. I never can see her face. I don't see her face unless I get up to where I can kiss her."

Still, Mrs. Kerrigan was thrilled to be able to watch Nancy skate for the national championship. "This is so exciting, but nerve-wracking at the same time," Nancy's mother had said before the competition began. "I'm just hoping for the best."

Nancy opened her long program with a jump called a double Axel. It was a simple jump, one she had done hundreds of times in practice without a mistake. But here at the nationals, with thousands of people watching, she fell. Quickly, she got back onto her feet and blocked out the demons in her head that wanted to tell her "You are so *hopeless.*" Nancy went on to skate an otherwise perfect routine, and the crowd gave her a standing ovation.

"Television can't possibly show what it was really like in that building," coach Mary Scotvold said afterwards. "The place turned around so much."

After her fall, Nancy said, "I told myself, 'You've trained for this. You can fix what you've done.' I fought back and ended up skating a good program."

The judges rewarded her effort with scores of 5.6, and two 5.7's, out of a possible 6.0. When the final tallies were in, Nancy's total score put her in third place. She had won the bronze medal and would be going to her first world championships! Nancy's teammates on the U.S. team would be Tonya and Kristi, who finished 1–2 at nationals.

Kristi had skated a very good program that night, but had slipped from first to second place after Tonya let loose with a gutsy routine that a reporter from *The Boston Globe* called "the most electrifying performance in the history of American women's figure skating."

Tonya won the title, her first, by landing all seven of her triple jumps, including a triple Axel—three-and-a-half complete twists in the air. It was the first time a

*W*hen she was a kid, one of Nancy's two older brothers called her "Ug," short for ugly! Today, Nancy doesn't take her good looks for granted.

*N*ancy spun to a fourth-place finish at the 1990 national championships, after having been fifth the year before. She improved every year and won the title in 1993.

*N*ancy's elegant style helped her win a bronze
medal at the '92 Olympics in Albertville, France.

𝒩ancy has always received great support from her parents, Brenda and Dan. Her father used to drive her to practice at 4:30 A.M.

𝒩ancy's mother, who is legally blind, watched her daughter's Olympic routine on a TV monitor especially set up for her.

*G*old-medal winner Kristi Yamaguchi was Nancy's roommate in the Olympic Village in '92. They get along well, on and off the ice.

*N*ancy and Olympic silver medalist Paul Wylie are good friends. They skated together in a stunning exhibition at Albertville.

*K*nown for her graceful skating, Nancy has worked to become a skater who can do dramatic jumps as well.

*N*ancy won the national championships in '93, but rival Tonya Harding (second from right) didn't place in the top three.

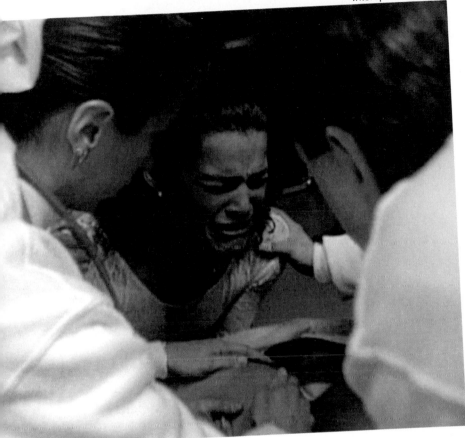

A frightening attack on Nancy before the 1994 national championships in Detroit left her knee injured and her Olympic hopes threatened.

*J*ust 11 days after the attack, Nancy's courage and determination allowed her to get back on the ice and continue her training for the Olympics.

woman from the United States had landed a triple Axel in competition. (She is still the only American to have landed one.) The judges rewarded Tonya that afternoon with eight marks of 5.9 and one perfect 6.0 for technical merit.

The 1991 world championships would be held in March in Munich, Germany. Nancy was excited about flying to Munich to compete with Tonya and Kristi in her first world championships. But even she didn't expect the event to be as dramatic as it turned out to be!

Tonya was favored to win the 1991 world title, because of her great performance at the U.S. nationals. Kristi was also expected to win a medal. The other favorite was Midori Ito *[EE-toe]*, an exciting 21-year-old skater from Japan. Midori was the only woman, besides Tonya, to have landed a triple Axel in competition.

A reporter from *The New York Times* wrote that if those three skaters "do not share the victory podium, it would be a surprise of major proportion."

Midori, however, had recently spent 18 days in a hospital after having two cysts removed from her throat. (A cyst is a kind of blister.) Another possible medal challenger was Surya Bonaly *[bone-a-LEE]* of France. Surya is an incredibly athletic skater, who can do back flips on the ice and has landed a quadruple jump in practice.

"Nancy Kerrigan, the third member of the United

States team," the *Times* reported, "is strictly a long shot."

Some people were more optimistic about Nancy's chances. One of them was Paul Wylie, the future Olympic silver medalist, who is a good friend of Nancy's and who also trained with Evy and Mary Scotvold.

"Nancy has always been in the top five in free skating [the long program], and last year she came so close it was a shame," he told a reporter. "She has the style. She is able to turn her program into drama. Kristi isn't able to do it in the same way. Midori and Tonya are very gifted, of course, but they don't have the same drama.

"[Nancy] is not just skating from one end of the rink to the other, putting in triples for the accountants," Paul added. "Emotion and aesthetics [beauty] are a strong part of her program. She's got a good chance."

Other observers also began to notice Nancy. Some remarked that Nancy's skating style was similar to that of world champion Jill Trenary. Both skaters, they said, were athletic enough to try difficult jumps, yet were also graceful and feminine enough to please judges who preferred to reward skaters for ballet-like movement rather than acrobatic tricks.

Nancy's coaches expected Nancy to finish anywhere between third and fifth. "She is incredibly fluid," said

Mrs. Scotvold of Nancy. "She has a marvelous sense of her body. She is very elegant, and people love it."

Going into the final afternoon of competition, Kristi was first, Tonya was second, Midori was third, and Nancy was fourth. But the battle for the world championship was far from over.

In the long program event, Tonya had a difficult time. She landed another triple Axel, but completed only three of her other six triple jumps. She finished second. "I didn't deserve to win," she said.

Kristi did deserve to win—and she did—after successfully landing six triples. The judges gave her an amazing seven 5.9's and one perfect 6.0 for artistic impression.

That left third place open—but for whom?

Midori started to have trouble on the ice even before the competition began. During warm-ups, she crashed into another skater and ended up with badly bruised ribs.

Then, after completing a combination triple Lutz/ double toe loop jump in her short program, Midori accidentally hurtled over a foot-high barrier that was protecting an ice-level television camera. Skating in her long program with pain in both her ribs and her left ankle, Midori landed only four of eight triples. She ended up in fourth place.

Nancy skated onto the ice, dressed in a beautiful black dress. Music from the movie, *Born on the Fourth of July*, filled the arena. Nancy fell once during her program, but skated well otherwise. When the judges' votes were in, she had moved ahead of Midori in the final standings to finish third.

Nancy had medaled in the first world championships she'd ever competed in!

For the first time in the history of women's figure skating, one country had swept the singles medals at the world championships!

Photographs of Kristi, Tonya, and Nancy, beaming with wide smiles and wearing medals around their necks, appeared in newspapers all over the country. "We're all still floating on cloud nine," Kristi said.

6 The Olympic Moment

Winning bronze medals at the 1991 national and world championships was just the start for Nancy. When she unpacked from her exciting trip to Germany, she knew that the Olympics were less than a year away. And she knew that she, Nancy Kerrigan, had a real shot at representing her country there!

The 1991 season "was a tremendous boost in confidence for Nancy," said coach Evy Scotvold. "It showed her that she had the talent, the material, the flair, and that the judges recognized her. It also showed her that she could deal with problems [like missed jumps and falls during a performance], block them out, and just skate.

"When she is skating well, she is so beautiful to watch," Mr. Scotvold said. "Maybe she needed to convince herself of that, and I think that happened [in 1991]."

Nancy knew it was not going to be easy to stay in the top three. She would have to stay sharp, and in shape, while she waited for the competitive season to start up again in the fall.

To stay in shape, Nancy follows a strict schedule of weight training, stretching, and four or five hours of daily skating. When the weather is warm, she bikes and works out on in-line skates to keep up her stamina.

Even after she was becoming a world-class figure skater, Nancy was known to chip away with her brothers in pickup hockey games a few blocks from their home. "One of my brothers helps run the Stoneham rink," Nancy told a reporter. "We would get big games going after eleven P.M., after the rink closed to the public. I'm just a hacker, but you should see me play hockey in my figure skates."

But in the summer of 1991, Nancy had to stop skating. She had developed tendinitis in both ankles, which made skating too painful. (Tendinitis is a soreness in the tendons, the body tissue that connects the muscles to the bones.) Nancy also was feeling pain in her back and neck. To get herself feeling well and back up on her skates, she began working with a physical therapist.

"I tried to skate several times last summer," Nancy

said later, "but it hurt so much that I ended up crying and going home. But I got better. Now I wear cushions and pads in my skates, and my feet don't hurt anymore."

By January 1992, Nancy was ready to compete at the 1992 national championships, which would be held in January in Orlando, Florida. At the nationals, Nancy had the support of some 40 relatives and friends who had made the trip from the Boston area to watch her perform.

Traveling 1,100 miles to watch someone skate a 2-minute 40-second short program and a 4-minute long program may seem a bit crazy, but to the close-knit Kerrigan family, it wasn't strange at all.

Nancy did not let her family down. At the nationals, Nancy continued her impressive climb up the figure-skating ladder. Her performance was not flawless—she missed three of seven planned triples in her long program—but she finished second to Kristi Yamaguchi, who won her first national title.

Kristi had been a runner-up for three years in a row, but this time she skated a very strong program. Nancy placed just ahead of defending champion Tonya Harding. The United States could send three skaters to the 1992 Winter Olympics in Albertville, France, and Nancy —along with Kristi and Tonya—had earned one of those spots. She would be on the U.S. Olympic team!

"I really worked hard to earn my place on the U.S. team," said Nancy a few weeks later. She admitted that she had felt more nervous about competing in the nationals than she did about her upcoming debut in the Olympics. "Now that I have a place on the team, the pressure is not as intense. I feel ready to compete. My training is going well. And I'm going to try to go to France and enjoy the experience and have fun. When I've taken that attitude in the past, things seem to work out."

A week before she flew to France, Nancy was the special guest performer at an ice show called Skating '92, which featured 1984 and 1988 Olympic gold medalist Katarina Witt of Germany and 1988 Olympic champion Brian Boitano of the United States.

The show was being held at the Boston Garden, an historic arena that is located only about 10 miles from her hometown. Naturally, Nancy had many friends and family members in the audience.

"But what made it so exciting," she said, "was when I came out to take my bow, everyone in the audience was standing up and clapping. I thought, 'Wow, this is really cool. They like me.' "

One thing Nancy discovered that she did *not* like was all the attention she was getting from newspaper and television reporters. Nancy is usually very shy with people she doesn't know, and she doesn't like to be interviewed about her private life.

Even her mother, who is more comfortable talking to people than Nancy is, was beginning to feel overwhelmed. "The phone hasn't stopped ringing since we returned from the national championships," Mrs. Kerrigan said. "And people tell us it's only going to get worse if things go well in France. It's all been so confusing. We aren't used to this."

Still, as the Olympics neared, the Kerrigan family got caught up in the excitement. Mrs. Kerrigan sometimes got so emotional about her daughter's upcoming trip that tears would well up in her eyes. "I never dreamed it would be like this," she said. "The whole thing is so mind-boggling. I use the word at least 10,000 times a day, but all I can say is 'Wow.' Just 'Wow!'

"At the worlds, that's when we started thinking that Nancy had a chance to make the Olympics," her mother added. "When I was Nancy's age, New Hampshire was the farthest away from home I'd ever been. But last year, Dan and I went to Munich [Germany] for the worlds, and now we're [going to] the Olympics!"

Nancy's family was able to travel to Albertville to cheer her on, thanks to a "Celebrate the Dream" grant given to them by the U.S. Postal Service. This is a program to help the families of athletes travel overseas to watch them compete at the Olympics.

The Kerrigans looked forward to Nancy's Olympic experience. Even though Mrs. Kerrigan's eyesight is poor, and she wouldn't be able to pick Nancy out of the crowd, she knew how she would react when the Olympic opening ceremony began. "I will be watching and I know I am going to cry," Mrs. Kerrigan said. "It's so big. So big."

Competing in the Olympics _was_ big. Nancy didn't want to get overwhelmed thinking about it. It helped her to have several good friends around while she was getting ready for the Games. One of those friends was sometime training partner Paul Wylie, who was competing in the Olympics for the second time. Paul and Nancy enjoyed being at the Games at the same time, and after the Olympic medals competition, they would skate together in a special exhibition.

"Nancy needed to escape from the pressure," Paul said later. "All I told her was she should withdraw a bit into herself, and in her own way get ready without distractions. I told her to wear a Walkman and listen to music and relax with soothing thoughts.

"I didn't say, 'Calm down,'" he added. "I tried to tell her things that would help her rather than playing with her mind."

Paul's skating career had often been a frustrating one, but he surprised everyone by winning a silver medal at the 1992 Games. His success helped Nancy's concentration, as well. "After Paul won, it made me realize that all of the work and dedication can pay off if you concentrate on it. If you can block out everything and put together a program that fits you and you have confidence in it, you will be rewarded."

Another person who helped Nancy relax was one of her biggest rivals—Kristi Yamaguchi—who had become one of her closest friends over the years. "Kristi is one of my best friends, and we get along so well," Nancy said. "I'm not sure what it would be like if she wasn't here. I've become so used to having her around."

The two skaters had first started to compete against each other when they were teenagers, and that's when Kristi and other skaters came up with an unusual nickname for Nancy. They called her "Para," which was short for "Paranoid," because Nancy was always asking whether she looked okay. "Does this go?" she would ask. "Does this skirt go with this shirt? Do I look okay?"

Nancy and Kristi asked U.S. team organizers to let them be roommates at the Olympic Village.

"It's great rooming with Kristi," said Nancy at the time. "Once we're away from the ice, we talk about other things, people we meet. It's relaxing and fun."

"I think it definitely helps rooming with Nancy," agreed Kristi. "We're here for the same thing, and we have the same goals. Away from the ice we don't think too much about skating. We just try to enjoy the athletes' village and the atmosphere."

Nancy added that competing against one another

never gets in the way of their friendship. "She does her job," Nancy said. "I do my job. We have no control of how the judges vote. We all support each other. Last month, we told Kristi to go out and make it tough for us [at the 1992 nationals]. She did."

Some of the reporters covering the Olympics did not know much about Nancy's skating ability, partly because she had popped up into world view only in the last year. But those who had seen her skate at the 1991 world championships could see that she had improved a lot since then, both athletically and artistically.

An article in *The New York Times* said: "Artistically Kristi has no match in the world, and of all the other leading skaters only Nancy comes close."

Former Olympic ice dancer Tracy Wilson, who was a commentator for CBS television at the figure skating events, said, "Nancy is a very elegant skater. She's also become quite a fighter. In the past, she used to get down on herself if she was off. Now, if she misses a jump, she'll fight back and still skate well."

Going into the Olympic competition, experts believed that all three U.S. skaters had excellent chances of winning medals. Only Midori Ito of Japan was considered a threat to another American sweep.

Nancy recalled later that when she stepped onto the ice to skate her short program that first night, "I wanted to feel like I'd been there before, like it was my own ice and the rink was like home. But I saw the Olympic flag and I said, 'The time is now.'"

Twenty-nine women made the final cut. After the short program, Kristi was in first place, Nancy was second, Surya Bonaly of France was third, and Midori was fourth.

Nancy had two days to get nervous about her long program, which would decide her fate in the Olympics. But, again, she was able to remain fairly calm. "I might have had problems with that situation in the past," she said. "But having so much support gave me confidence and helped me focus on what I wanted to do."

One thing Nancy refused to let herself do was think about winning the gold. "I've done that before," she said. "It kind of freaked me out. I don't bother doing that anymore. Medals aren't everything."

Nancy's program was ambitious. It featured seven triple jumps, including a triple toe loop, a triple Lutz, a triple flip, and a triple Salchow.

Once again skating to music from the movie, *Born on the Fourth of July*, Nancy glided gracefully around the Olympic arena looking radiant in a white skating dress.

Early in her performance, Nancy missed a triple jump combination and singled a triple Lutz. But, thanks to the way she had learned to keep herself calm in stressful situations, she did not let the rest of her performance fall apart. "It really didn't affect me that much," Nancy recalled. "I wasn't thinking about being perfect, just about presenting my program and letting whatever would happen happen."

She touched the ice on a triple toe loop near the end of her routine, but she earned decent marks from the judges for her overall performance. Now there was nothing to do but wait and see how the remaining skaters did.

Kristi was sitting fairly comfortably in first place by then. But the other two medal spots were up for grabs. Would Nancy edge out at least two of the three other leading contenders: Midori, Surya, or Tonya?

By the time Midori's scores were flashed up on the scoreboard, the Kerrigan family had forgotten what Nancy's final score had been. Because of her three mistakes, they assumed she had finished fourth. But Nancy's Uncle William had seen the results on the screen, and he straightened the family out: Nancy had finished _third!_ She had won a bronze medal in the Olympics!

It had been 32 years since two American women had won medals in the same Olympic singles competition. But that night, two United States flags were hoisted above the rink as the United States national anthem was played in honor of the first-place finish of Nancy's good friend Kristi. Midori stood on the second-place podium. Tonya, the third member of the American team, had finished fourth.

Sixteen years earlier, Nancy had been one of hundreds of little girls who took to the ice wanting to be an Olympic champion some day—and look how close she had come!

7 Champion at Last

When Nancy returned to Massachusetts after the Olympics, she was treated like a hero.

Stoneham city officials decided to host Nancy Kerrigan Day on March 8, 1992. They held a two-hour parade in her honor, which included dozens of floats, marching bands, and antique cars. Nancy, sitting in the back of a convertible, waved to the people who lined the parade route. There were more than 40,000 people there to greet her!

Later in the day, a full house of 2,000 people filled the nearby Unicorn arena—where Nancy had taken some of her earliest skating lessons—to watch her perform in a demonstration. After Nancy's show, members of the audience stood and held up signs that read "6.0," to let her know that they thought her skating was perfect. The crowd gave her a standing ovation.

"They thought she was just fantastic," said one city official.

The street that leads to the Unicorn arena was re-named Kerrigan Way. And a dinner and dance were held in Nancy's honor later that night.

"It's [difficult to remember] when something this important and enjoyable was done in such a positive way," said another city official. "In this day and age when we have all the negatives to deal with, it's nice to have such a positive, high day, and over something as pleasant as Nancy Kerrigan.

"[What Nancy has done is] an American dream," the official added. "She comes from a working-class family. Only in America could something like this happen."

The day was tremendous fun for Nancy, too. "I had a great time," she said. "It's a little overwhelming. It's great to see how many people are behind me, supporting me."

Nancy didn't have time to rest on her laurels, though. The world championships were coming up quickly.

The 1992 worlds were held in Oakland, California, two weeks after Nancy Kerrigan Day was celebrated in Stoneham. Nancy went into the competition with high hopes.

When it was her turn to skate, Nancy did not put on a great performance—she fell once and had several shaky jumps, including a triple Lutz that she turned into a single Lutz. Still, she completed a program that was highly artistic and difficult enough to lift her into second place overall. It was the highest finish Nancy had ever had in a major world competition!

Kristi Yamaguchi, as expected, was able to defend her world title. A newcomer, 15-year-old Lu Chen of China, won the bronze. It was the first time a skater from China had ever won a medal at skating's world championships. Kristi's and Nancy's teammate, Tonya Harding, struggled, and fell to sixth place.

For Kristi, her second world title capped off a perfect year. She had become the first United States woman since Peggy Fleming in 1968 to win back-to-back world championships. After winning the 1992 nationals, Kristi had become the first U.S. woman since Dorothy Hamill in 1976 to win the Olympic gold medal. What could the 20-year-old skater do to top that?

Kristi decided that the only thing left to do with her career was to turn professional, which would enable her to earn money skating in ice shows. In September, Kristi announced her retirement from amateur skating.

"One of the toughest things about this decision," Kristi said, "was knowing I'd be leaving Nancy. Having Nancy around has always been a comfort zone for me. I know that she'll be okay and will do very well without me. I'd like very much for her to succeed me as world champion."

Nancy wanted that, as well. She had been pleased with her performance at the nationals, Olympics, and worlds in 1992, but she felt that she still hadn't reached her potential as a skater. She was doing well in spite of her mistakes. Imagine how well she could do if she could eliminate those mistakes, she wondered. Nancy intended to work even harder in training. "I believe I can improve on my skating and my performance," she said.

Nancy also hoped that her life would get back to normal: skating, spending time with her family, and not doing much else. But once Nancy's skating success, photogenic good looks, and sweet personality became known outside of Stoneham, she was quickly thrust under a national spotlight.

"Was I naive!" Nancy said. "I thought all the attention would be done, but it was only just starting. The interviews, the spooohoo, the commercials. I wouldn't trade any of it, but it's been hectic!"

She earned $50,000 by winning a competition that included professional and amateur skaters later in the year. Six companies, including Reebok, Seiko, Northwest Airlines, and Campbell's soup, paid her to promote their products. (According to Olympic rules, the money she earned had to go into a special fund to pay her training costs. That way she could keep her status as an amateur and be eligible to compete in the Olympics and other international and national competitions.)

Nancy's agent, Jerry Solomon, whose company also represents athletes like tennis player Gabriela Sabatini and swimmer Janet Evans, called her with an evergrowing list of places she needed to be and people who wanted to meet with her.

Nancy was on the cover of the 1992 year-end issue of _Life_ magazine. In 1993, she was named one of _People_ magazine's "50 Most Beautiful People in the World." _The Boston Globe_ called her "America's ice queen and poster girl."

One reporter asked Nancy if she knew why people around the country were so interested in her now. She shrugged off the question, saying, "I guess it's because I've been on TV a lot."

"She hates this," said her dad, of all the attention Nancy was receiving. "But she's handling it great."

Someone asked her what had changed the most in her life since the Olympics. "Oh, just _everything_," she said.

Soon it was time for Nancy to live up to what everyone was saying and writing about her. In January, she would be competing in the 1993 national championships, which would be held in Phoenix, Arizona.

When Nancy arrived in Phoenix, she knew that she

was now the favored skater of the bunch, the one who was expected to win the championship. In Nancy's first year of competition at the nationals, back in 1988, Debi Thomas was the star. After that it was Jill Trenary. Then Tonya Harding and Kristi Yamaguchi. Of that group, only Tonya was still competing.

Nancy really missed Kristi. They had competed against each other since 1985, when they were both junior-level skaters. "It seems strange not to have her here," Nancy said.

It also seemed strange to Nancy to find herself surrounded by good skaters who were much younger than she was. She had been 18 when she first made it to the senior nationals. Now, at age 23, "I'm competing against a twelve-year-old," she said with amazement, referring to Michelle Kwan (who ended up finishing sixth).

When Nancy moved up to senior competition, five years earlier, she had finished 12th at the nationals. The year after that she had been fifth, then fourth a year later, then third. In 1992, she had finished second. Could she continue her climb by taking that one last step? Could she win her first national title in 1993?

"I haven't been thinking about that," she insisted. "I'm just concentrating on what I have to do. The last few weeks my coaches have had the whip out. I go through my entire program, then go to rewind, push 'play' and do it again. I'm more relaxed each time. For me, that's real important."

She did admit, though, that it was tough to deal with the fact that most people expected her to win. "I tried not to worry about the pressures of being the favored one," she said.

The only serious threat to Nancy's chances for a gold medal was Tonya.

Unlike Nancy, Tonya had had a difficult year of competition in 1992. An ankle injury had made it tough to complete the jumps she was famous for, particularly the triple Axel. She had gotten married at age 19 in 1990 to a man named Jeff Gillooly, and some people believed that strains in their marriage had taken its toll on her. She also was struggling to lose extra pounds she had gained.

After putting in the spectacular performance that had wowed judges in 1991, Tonya had finished third at the nationals in 1992, fourth at the Olympics, and sixth at the 1992 worlds. But she said she was ready to take on Nancy for the 1993 title. "I'm coming in the same way I did in 1991," Tonya said, referring to the year she had won the nationals. "Nobody expects anything."

But Tonya's struggles were not over, it seemed. As soon as she made her approach for the first jump in her short program, Tonya's dress came undone. A snap on her halter popped open, forcing her to stop her routine and ask for a restart. She started again, nailed all of her jumps, and moved into second place.

Then, Tonya caught a head cold before the final round of competition began. Coupled with the asthma she has suffered with since she was a child, Tonya had trouble breathing during her performance. She missed three triples, and ended up finishing fourth in the tournament.

In fact, few of the top skaters looked good. Nicole Bobek, 15, and Tonia Kwiatkowski, 21, skated well, but not great. Only 15-year-old Lisa Ervin finished her long program without falling.

"Nobody had done anything," said coach Evy Scotvold. "And Nancy knew that."

Nancy was in first place after the short program. She looked stunning in a black skating dress, as she stepped onto the ice—her long program to music from the movie, *Beauty and the Beast*. But she was nervous inside. She faltered on the first two jumps before pulling herself together. "What I've learned is that if I fall in the beginning, I have to leave it there and not let it snowball," she said.

Though she landed only three of the six triples she had planned, no one else was a match for Nancy artistically and technically. The judges had no trouble awarding her the highest scores of the tournament.

Nancy was the 1993 national champion!

She was happy with her gold medal, but not entirely thrilled with her performance. "I could have skated better, but I was happy with where it put me," she said. "I left some room for myself to improve in the worlds."

The United States Olympic Committee named Nancy as its SportsWoman of the Month for January 1993. After the announcement, Nancy was interviewed by several reporters. One of them asked Nancy to talk about why so many of the American women had fallen during the nationals.

Nancy said that one reason might be that there is more pressure every year to complete at least six triples in the long program. "I don't think a lot of the girls are ready to do that and be consistent with it yet," she said. "It is hard to keep your concentration for four minutes and do so many major things in one routine. When there weren't as many triple jumps in the programs, you didn't see as many falls or mistakes."

In some cases, she said, young skaters can get by with attempting fewer triples, because there is less pressure on them to put together a polished program. But veteran skaters are expected to make more jumps. "I would rather watch someone doing three or four triples and look very well presented," Nancy said, "rather than all these jumps here and there." Nancy was speaking as a veteran of many skating competitions and, now, a champion.

The 1993 world championships would be held in March in Prague, in the Czech Republic. As the United States team prepared to travel to Europe, some U.S. skating experts were worried that the U.S. women might have trouble earning a medal there. They weren't sure that Nancy or her teammates were mentally strong enough to put in the kind of performance they would need against the emerging European stars, like France's Surya Bonaly. Nancy's U.S. teammates, second-place finisher Lisa Ervin and bronze medalist Tonia Kwiatkowski, were newcomers to the pressure of the world championships.

If the team didn't bring home at least one medal, international rules stated that the United States would be able to send only two skaters to the 1994 Olympics. Countries with medal-winning skaters in the previous worlds are entitled to enter three skaters at the Games.

Nancy was asked if she was nervous about carrying that responsibility. "I don't think I should take that pressure on myself," Nancy said "Although I would be happy to be the one that would allow more skaters to go next year, I really want to go and just think about my skating. If I do what I can, there is a good chance that I will get one of those spots. We'll just have to see."

Other skating observers pointed out that American skaters had done well at the world championships in recent years, winning the gold medal three years in a

row. Jill Trenary had won it in 1990, and Kristi Yamaguchi had won it the following two years. Nancy had
finished third at the 1991 worlds, and second in 1992.
Could she, as she had in the nationals, climb that last
step up the ladder and finish first in 1993?

"If she can do the program she does every day," said
Mr. Scotvold, "she'll win."

The pressure was on Nancy to perform well. And the
pressure was intense.

8 Back From a Fall

When the 1993 world championships began in Prague, Nancy felt she was up to the challenge of showing that she was now the best female figure skater in the world.

Nancy would be the 17th of 24 skaters to perform in the short-program competition. Waiting behind the rink for her turn to skate, she heard the crowd cheer loudly for Josée Chouinard of Canada, another medal contender. But she didn't know what kind of scores the other skaters were receiving from the judges.

"To tell you the truth, I didn't pay attention to what was happening before I skated," she said later. "I figured that I had to do what I had to do."

Nancy skated cleanly and smoothly in her short program and moved into first place. Only unknown newcomer Oksana Baiul [by-OOL], a 15-year-old from the

Ukraine, seemed hot on her trail. Surya Bonaly of France was a comfortable distance behind Nancy and Oksana in points.

"It was easy today, it felt good," Nancy told a reporter after her performance. "I have more than just the jumps, and I think that makes a difference. But a lot of others here do, too. That's good to see."

Once again, people everywhere were saying that Nancy was the skater to beat. But Nancy knew it wouldn't be that easy. "You can get a feel sometimes by the way the crowd responds, how they cheer when they see or hear your name, and that can be a big boost," she said. "But it all comes down to the judges and who skates well."

Coach Evy Scotvold knew that Nancy had not won anything yet. "If you want to win it, you have to win the long [program]," he said. "That's where Nancy is strongest. There was a lot of good talent out there. Now we'll see who can do it for four minutes."

Oksana skated before Nancy. In her first world competition, Oksana thrilled the audience and judges with her long program. She completed five triple jumps, and earned scores ranging from 5.6 to 5.9. Surya also skated before Nancy, and she also skated well, landing *seven* triples. The competition was tight, but Nancy still had a chance to stay on top—if she nailed her routine.

Nancy skated out onto the ice and into the spotlight,

wearing a pink skating outfit, with her hair pulled back and tied with a pink bow. She seemed as if she had everything together. But it didn't take long before it all began to fall apart.

Only 27 seconds into her long program, Nancy's right hand touched the ice at the end of a triple flip. Then, about 10 seconds later, she gave up on a triple Lutz attempt and settled for a single. Twenty seconds after that, Nancy's knees buckled shakily while landing a triple Salchow. She shorted two other jumps that were supposed to be triples into doubles, and took an unwanted step in the middle of a jump combination.

Nancy skated off the ice with her head down. She was crushed. While she waited for her scores to be announced, a very unhappy Nancy told her coaches, "I just want to die." She turned to coach Mary Scotvold, and asked, "Can I do it again?" The answer, of course, was no.

The judges had no choice but to give Nancy low scores, which sent her toppling from first place to fifth place. There was to be no medal at the 1993 worlds for Nancy, or for any other American skaters.

Immediately after her performance, Mr. Scotvold said Nancy told him that "she was disgusted with herself. She said 'I stink. I should be on the podium. What in the world did I do?' "

Oksana was the one to win the gold medal, becoming

the youngest world champion since Sonja Henie of Norway won in 1927. Surya finished second, and China's Lu Chen won the bronze medal for the second year in a row.

"I don't know, it just wasn't my day," Nancy said, fighting back tears at a press conference later. "I worked really hard and didn't expect anything like that. The knees just weren't working, I guess. I felt more pressure than I admitted. I hope people realize it makes me human."

Mrs. Scotvold said she hoped this defeat would make Nancy a better skater. "I don't know one skater who hasn't had a devastating, horrendous experience," she said. "Usually it makes them stronger. They're so humiliated, they can't leave it like that."

Mr. Scotvold agreed. He also said that being considered the top skater is a pressure-packed position, something Nancy had not gotten used to. "She was leading the pack, she was the favorite, and this was something she had never done before," he said. "I think she'll be better for this."

Nancy's friend Paul Wylie offered a skater's point of view. "After the Olympic year, there is such a letdown," he said. "[Nancy] was so high, riding an incredible crest, and all of a sudden a new skater [Oksana] came from nowhere. It surprised her, demoralized her."

Mr. Scotvold said Nancy had experienced the bad

day of all bad days, but that she could bounce back. "If I didn't think she could come back stronger for this, that she couldn't handle it, then I wouldn't let her do it," he said. "I know Nancy, and she's a tough fighting skater."

But before she could come back, Nancy was to be dealt one more blow. That happened at the Hershey's Kisses Pro-Am Championships in Los Angeles in April, which is a competition that includes amateurs and professionals. Nancy once again was the leader after the first round, but then she fell three times in the final round. She finished a disappointing second to 1988 Olympian Caryn Kadavy.

"Obviously I've hit a pretty big low," Nancy said after the competition. "There is nowhere for me to go but up. It's going to be hard, but I know I'm capable of doing it."

"She has a confidence problem right now," said Mr. Scotvold. Even with her harsh lesson at the worlds, he added, "I think she only half believed it. If she doesn't get the picture now, she never will."

Bouncing back was not going to happen overnight, however. Nancy was angry with herself, and afraid of failing. By June, she was struggling with Mr. Scotvold at practice. She wouldn't do a complete run-through of her four-minute routine. She wasn't lazy, but sometimes she would purposely leave out a spin or a jump. Something was bothering Nancy, and it was something that was hard for her to explain to anyone, even her coaches.

Finally, Mr. Scotvold threw up his hands, quit as her coach, and left her solely in the hands of his wife for one month. "It was enormously frustrating," he says. "Nancy was totally distracted."

Nancy knew that her post-Olympic year had gone from "poor to terrible to horrific." To help find the reasons why, she began working with Cindy Adams, a sports psychologist. A psychologist is an expert in the workings of the mind. He or she helps people to understand why they do the things they do. Ms. Adams was a former figure skater who understood Nancy's sport and how hard it was to become a world champion.

Through talking with Ms. Adams, Nancy began to learn what made her tick as a person and how that affected her on the ice. She learned that she was driven to succeed, not because she wanted to win, but because she was afraid of losing. Even in practice she had always held something back.

"It's kind of scary, giving everything you have," Nancy says now. "What if you're not as good as you think you are?"

"I call it 'The Voice,' " says Paul Wylie, meaning a little voice in your head that tells you that you can't do something. "It's that sense of doubt that creeps in and doesn't let go. You have to learn to quiet that voice."

After taking a week off in July, Nancy turned her attention to the 1993–1994 skating season by getting even more serious about her skating career. In some ways, she told reporters later, finishing so poorly in the worlds "might have been the best thing for me. I was mad at myself. It made me fight harder."

Nancy now realized that there was no coasting to success. She had to fight for what she wanted and give it all she had. "We were just hoping to get through last year without a disaster, and it didn't happen," recalls Mr. Scotvold. "It didn't take a lot to convince her changes needed to be made."

The first change: Nancy cut down on the outside commitments that had occupied so much of her time the previous year: the endorsements, the skating shows, the appearances. "I like to be busy, but it affected me a lot more than I thought it would," she admits. "I was taking plane rides to different places all the time and it was a great experience, but I had to go back to concentrating on my skating. If I don't skate well, they won't want me anymore."

She also worked to lose four pounds, and exercised with the videotape called, *Abs of Steel*. Nancy is 5'4" tall. She wanted to get her weight down to 111 pounds to make it that much easier to get high off the ground on her triple jumps.

And she started to run through her program seven

or eight times a day, six days a week. As Mr. Scotvold recalled, she had never done one perfect run in the eight years he had been her coach, but now he was starting to see her skate flawless programs in practice. And, importantly, her off-days did not get her down like they used to.

"The last few years I was really afraid to put the music on at practice," Nancy says. "If I wasn't perfect I'd get mad at myself, put myself down. It's crazy. I'm not a bad person if I have a bad day."

Nancy was taking the extra steps to mold herself into a champion. "Nancy is finally skating the way she should have been the past two years," said Mr. Scotvold just before the 1993–94 season began. "Her consistency and focus are the best they have been."

The new Nancy Kerrigan was to be unveiled in October 1993 at the Piruetten international figure skating competition in Hamar, Norway, on the rink that would be the site of the 1994 Olympic skating events. Three of the four women who had beaten her at 1993 world championships would be competing at the event: Surya Bonaly, Lu Chen, and Yuka Sato of Japan. Only reigning world champion Oksana Baiul would be missing from the action.

It was to be Nancy's first big confidence test after the 1993 worlds. Would she pass?

9 *Danger in Detroit*

Nancy was looking forward to the Piruetten international competition in Norway in October 1993 because it would give her a chance to show the world that her skating was back on track. And the fact that the competition would be held at the site of the 1994 Winter Olympic skating competition—the Hamar Olympic Amphitheatre near Lillehammer, Norway—made it even more exciting.

When the competition began, Nancy skated confidently in her short program. Though she fell once, her performance was impressive enough to land her in second place after the first day of competition. Then, in the final round, she skated beautifully in the long program.

Nancy's new long program routine, skated to music written by singer/songwriter Neil Diamond and performed by the Boston Pops orchestra, included six triple jumps. Nancy had been working hard on her routine, and it showed. She nailed five of the six triples impressively.

But it was Nancy's artistic skill that especially impressed the judges. They awarded her six 5.9 scores in the artistic impression category, and that was enough to put Nancy over the top. She was the winner! Canada's Josée Chouinard and China's Lu Chen finished second and third respectively. Tonya Harding did not participate in the competition.

Nancy had bounced back with a stunning victory. "It felt great," she said afterward. "When doesn't it feel great to win? I was pretty excited and really confident. I'd been training hard and I felt ready to compete."

A month later, Nancy put herself to the test again. She competed with professional and amateur skaters at the AT&T Pro-Am Challenge, which was held in Philadelphia, Pennsylvania. In both her short and long programs, Nancy briefly lost her balance and touched her hand to the ice. But she did not lose her cool. Again, she finished first!

With two first-place finishes behind her, Nancy arrived in Detroit for the 1994 national championships in January with a mission: to put her disappointing performance at the 1993 worlds behind her, win a second consecutive national title, and let everyone know that she was the one to beat at the upcoming Olympics.

She was confident that she would succeed. In the past, other people had often predicted that Nancy would win an event, but she had never allowed herself to make the same prediction. Now she said, "I think I'm the favorite. I'm good enough. I know I'm good enough to win. I expect to win."

A few weeks before the nationals began, Nancy did three consecutive run-throughs of her long program. "And I hit seventeen of eighteen triples," she said proudly. "One time through the program seems easy now."

She skated her program over and over in practice, with very little rest in between. "I wouldn't let myself skip anything this year," she said. "I didn't want to get into that habit."

Even to her coaches, Nancy seemed to be a changed, more driven skater. "I have to tell her it's great what she's doing, but you can't expect six or eight perfect programs in one day," said coach Evy Scotvold. "It seems strange to be saying that to this young lady."

Nancy also was more relaxed than ever. She now listened to a cassette tape of comedy routines before competing to help her get rid of pre-skate jitters. "I've worked my butt off," she said, but she was also "having a lot of fun."

On Tuesday, January 4, three days before the nationals were to begin, Mr. Scotvold told reporters gathered in Detroit, "[Nancy has] never worked this hard before.

She's never done the run-throughs she's doing now. Double run-throughs. Going for perfect run-throughs. She's in fantastic shape. Her power is incredible. When she skates, she looks like she needs a bigger ice surface."

The next day, Nancy said, "I'm skating better than ever. I've worked for this a long time, and I've geared everything for this year. This should be my year."

Amid all that optimism, tragedy struck. After practice the next day, the man in the black hat came out of nowhere and clubbed Nancy above her right knee. One minute, Nancy was ready to conquer the skating world. The next minute, her hopes and dreams were in doubt.

"It's just horrifying," said Nancy's sister-in-law, Tammy Moscaritolo. "Why would anyone want to hurt Nancy?"

"We heard the news at about four P.M.," said the manager of the skating rink where Nancy practices when she is at home in Massachusetts. "There were several figure skaters on the ice at the time. Everyone came off the ice and flooded into the office. We made some phone calls [to Detroit] and found out what happened. We were all in a state of shock. Then the phone started ringing off the hook."

It seemed that the entire nation and much of the world was outraged by the attack on Nancy. Who would do such a thing? Immediately afterward, people began to speculate that perhaps a deranged fan of Tonya Harding's had attacked Nancy.

Many sports fans remembered that tennis star Monica Seles had been hurt the previous spring by a fan of Steffi Graf's. The fan, who was arrested on the spot, had wanted Monica out of the way so that Steffi could move back up to first place in the rankings. Tonya was Nancy's chief rival for the championship. Was someone trying to keep Nancy from competing so that Tonya could win the national title?

Others remembered that former Olympic figure skating champion Katarina Witt had been harassed by a fan several years earlier. The fan was eventually arrested and convicted after sending more than 50 frightening letters to Katarina.

Like many athletes in the public eye, Nancy, too, had reccivod letters that made her nervous. One of them was sent from an address in Ontario, Canada, which was just a few miles over the Canadian border from Detroit. As she was waiting to be taken to the hospital after the attack, Nancy remembered those letters. She told the police about them, in case they could be of some help in tracking down her attacker.

After Nancy was forced to withdraw from the nationals, because of the swelling and stiffness of her right knee, she was very upset. "I have been skating so well," she said. "I wanted to show everyone I didn't lose it.

I'm better now than I ever have been. I really wanted to do it for myself."

The police launched an immediate investigation into the attack. They began interviewing witnesses and other skaters, and studied a videotape taken at the time, which gave a fuzzy picture of the attacker making his escape. The Federal Bureau of Investigation (FBI) also began its own probe.

On January 10, a minister in Portland told the FBI that he had heard a tape recording of several men talking about a plot to hurt Nancy before the nationals. Two of the men speaking on the tape were believed to be Tonya Harding's ex-husband, Jeff Gillooly, and her bodyguard, Shawn Eric Eckardt, who lived in Portland. The minister said Shawn had made the tape and played it for him.

Tonya's ex-husband told reporters that he had no involvement in the attack. "That's illegal," he said. "I wouldn't do that. I have more faith in my wife than to bump off her competitors."

Her bodyguard said that it was "absurd" to think that he had had anything to do with the attack.

But the 26-year-old bodyguard later confessed to police that he was part of the plot. He was arrested and charged with conspiracy to commit assault, which is punishable by up to 10 years in jail and a fine of $100,000.

Police told reporters that the bodyguard said he had hired two men to pull off the attack. They also said he told them Tonya's ex-husband, allegedly motivated by the money she might earn if she were a national and Olympic champion, was the mastermind behind the plan.

On January 13, a 29-year-old man named Derrick Smith surrendered to the police in Phoenix, Arizona, where he lived. He was flown to the Portland airport and taken into custody by police. Authorities believed he was the driver of the getaway car after the attack.

On January 14, Derrick Smith's nephew, a 22-year-old man named Shane Stant, turned himself over to FBI investigators in Phoenix. He was arrested and accused of being the man who attacked Nancy with what turned out to be a telescoping police baton.

According to *The Boston Globe*, Stant told investigators that Tonya Harding herself had been involved in the conspiracy "way back." But the police did not know if he was telling the truth.

On January 18, Tonya was questioned by the FBI for 10 hours. During the questioning, she announced that she and Jeff Gillooly were separating. Having married in 1990, they divorced in August 1993, but had started living together again in September.

On January 20, Jeff Gillooly, 26, was arrested in Portland, where he and Tonya lived.

Although some of the suspects were pointing fingers at Tonya, the skater said that she had nothing to do with the plot to hurt Nancy.

Tonya's former agent, Michael Rosenberg, who represents 1993 world champion Oksana Baiul, told reporters after the arrests that he believed Tonya was innocent of the accusations that the arrested men were making. "Her competitive spirit is so strong, she wants her opponents to step up at their best," he said. "She doesn't want to hear people make excuses—a flu bug, an ankle sprain. No excuses. She wasn't jealous of Nancy. She looked past Nancy. Her number one rival is Oksana."

Tonya and Nancy had skated against each other 13 times in their careers; Tonya had come out on top six of those times. "If anyone wanted to compete against Nancy," Tonya said, "it was me."

On January 27, Tonya read a statement to the press that said that she had no knowledge of the attack before it happened, but that she did learn information about the assault afterward that she did not immediately tell to the police or the FBI. She said she hoped that her saying this would not result in her being removed from the Olympic team.

"I am embarrassed and ashamed to think that that anyone close to me could be involved," Tonya said. "I had no prior knowledge of the planned assault on

Nancy Kerrigan. I am responsible, however, for failing to report things I learned about the assault when I returned home from nationals. Many of you will be unable to forgive me for that. It will be difficult to forgive myself.

"Despite my mistakes and my rough edges, I have done nothing to violate the standards of excellence, of sportsmanship that are expected in an Olympic athlete," Tonya continued. "I have devoted my entire life to one objective: winning an Olympic gold medal for my country This is my last chance. I ask only for your understanding and the opportunity to represent my country with the best figure skating performance of my life."

On February 1, Jeff Gillooly pleaded guilty for his role in the attack on Nancy and told investigators that Tonya had approved of and helped plan the attack. Tonya, speaking through her lawyer, continued to deny that she was involved.

As the police went on with their investigation, the U.S. Figure Skating Association began to discuss whether Tonya should be allowed to stay on the Olympic team. They decided to take Michelle Kwan, the second-place finisher at the nationals, to Norway as a backup.

Meanwhile, Nancy turned her attention to the difficult task of regaining the strength and flexibility in her knee. The 1994 Olympics were only a few weeks away!

10 *Going for the Gold*

Three thousand miles away from the police and FBI investigations in Portland, Oregon, Nancy was back home in Stoneham, Massachusetts. She was concentrating on her own goal: to get back up on her skates as soon as possible.

Two days after the attack, Nancy said the swelling in her knee had already gone way down, and that she was able to move the knee much more easily.

The following Monday, Nancy had a special test on her knee to determine how badly it had been damaged. The test is called a magnetic resonance imaging test (MRI) and it allows the doctor to see inside a person's body to the muscles and bones. The test revealed that there was no hidden damage to her muscles or kneecap.

One doctor who examined Nancy said her knee was

dramatically improved. "At therapy," she said happily of the people who were working with her on her recovery, "they almost looked surprised."

Nancy started her rehabilitation with exercises in a swimming pool to strengthen her muscles gently, and then began workouts on a stationary bicycle. Nancy was working three hours a day on gentle hopping exercises, using 50 percent of her weight, to restore her muscle strength. Doctors were pleased with the smooth healing process of her knee. But the skater knew it would be dangerous to train too hard too fast. "Nancy has said, 'The knee's the boss,' " said her physical therapist, "and she's right."

She eased back into training slowly, first making jumps and rehearsing her routine on the floor of her parents' home. A few days after that, doctors said she could get back onto the ice, but that she was not allowed to try any jumps. "I think I'm going to be bored just skating around," she said. "But just to be out there will be nice."

By January 25, less than three weeks after the attack, Nancy was able to complete three-hour skating practices that included triple jumps. Then, by January 27, Nancy was able to skate her complete Olympic program at practice.

"She's doing her full practice every day, several times, with all the triple jumps," said coach Evy Scotvold. "I've had tears in my eyes watching her. Nancy's been making a heroic effort."

It seemed that Nancy's recovery from the physical injury would be complete before she took her place in Norway as a member of the U.S. Olympic team. But some people worried that it might take longer for her to recover from the emotional pain of the attack. As one sports psychologist said, "A bruise can do more damage to the psyche than to the bone."

Another sports psychologist pointed out that it took tennis star Monica Seles much longer to regain her mental strength, after being attacked by a crazed fan of Steffy Graf's, than to recover physically. As a top athlete, Monica "felt that nothing could harm her," said the psychologist. "The stabbing must have been devastating to her self-esteem."

The same day that Nancy was attacked, Monica pulled out of a major tennis tournament in Australia. It would have been her first competition since she was attacked eight months earlier. Monica later released a statement to the press that read: "Crimes against [celebrities] are more public, but not more tragic than what happens to too many innocent victims today. My thoughts are with Nancy, and I sympathize with the shock and horror she and other victims of senseless crimes experience."

Soon after the attack Nancy admitted, "I am a little

paranoid now. It's hard to say how long I'll look over my shoulder to see who is behind me."

Nancy told a reporter from *People* magazine that she had been at a party a few days after the attack and had been watching a little kid. "Suddenly I turned around, and there was someone standing with a bag of potato chips in their hand, close to my head," she recalled. "It scared me for a second, and I jumped."

Sometimes celebrities hire bodyguards to protect them, but Nancy's agent says that it is a solution most people hope they don't have to take. "I don't think athletes want bodyguards everywhere they go," the agent said. "Nancy Kerrigan wants to be a person. She wants to be able to have lunch in the hotel coffee shop and have fans ask for autographs. Athletes don't want to be off-limits to the whole world."

Just two days after the attack, in fact, Nancy sat in an otherwise deserted arena and signed autographs for hundreds of young fans for more than an hour. "Nancy might be fragile mentally when it comes to her skating," said coach Mary Scotvold to a *Sports Illustrated* reporter, "but she's a tough little girl off the ice. She's not as vulnerable as she might seem."

"I don't believe she needs any help to get over this," agreed her mother. "She's tough. She's strong. It's partly the way we brought her up."

Though Nancy did not want to hide from the whole

world, she didn't want to be in the public eye every day either. But with reporters camped outside her home, following her nearly everywhere, it was sometimes difficult to hold on to her privacy. The whole scene, thought Nancy, was also hilarious. Sometimes she amused herself by watching reporters through binoculars from inside the house.

"She just laughs," said Mr. Scotvold. "She thinks it's a farce, the craziest thing she's ever seen."

In one story, *The Boston Globe* wrote an account of a fairly typical day in Nancy's new life: Her father left the house at 8:30 A.M., ignored the reporters at the end of the driveway, and began to shovel snow. At 10 A.M., Nancy's brother Michael drove her to a club for a swimming workout, after a high-speed chase in which they tried to get away from the swarm of reporters who drove after them. At noon she was taken out a back door and driven to a local hospital for physical therapy. She returned home at 2:30 P.M., and left for a doctor's appointment three hours later.

Fans wanted to see Nancy, too. One local 11-year-old boy said his fifth-grade class made cards and wrote letters to Nancy. The cards were dropped off at her house, but it wasn't easy to get through. "The security was really tight," said the boy. "My friend said that the cops wouldn't let him walk past the camera people to give Nancy the cards."

Nancy received stacks of mail from people who wished her well in her recovery. One letter was from former President Ronald Reagan and his wife Nancy. It read: "We are so thankful you weren't harmed. We both know how difficult it can be to live in the public eye."

Even if Nancy were to survive the physical, mental, and media tests, one big question remained. The Olympic figure skating competition was scheduled to begin on February 23, 1994. With all of those distractions, would Nancy be able to skate the performance of her life when she stepped onto Olympic ice?

Mr. Scotvold wondered if all the support Nancy was receiving from fans would make her less angry about being attacked and too soft when she got onto the ice. Being a little angry might be a good thing, he said, because it could make her skate more fiercely at the Games.

And since so many people were now pulling for Nancy to win the gold medal, would the pressure be too great? "Nancy's going to have the [pressure] of [having] the world pulling for her," Mr. Scotvold said.

As the date for the Olympic competition drew closer, and other top skaters like Oksana Baiul, Surya Bonaly, and Lu Chen prepared for what they hoped would be the performances of *their* lives, Nancy felt confident. "I feel if my leg is strong enough to perform, I'll be strong enough," she said. "This is what I want to do. I want to prove I can do this. That all this work wasn't a waste."

Some sports business people predicted that many companies would pay Nancy a lot of money to promote their products if she did well at the Olympics. A bronze medal would be great, a silver medal would be even better, and if she were to win the medal that so many girls dream of—the gold—the rewards would be astounding.

"If Nancy wins the gold medal, she would be Dorothy Hamill, Peggy Fleming, and Katarina Witt rolled into one," said one sports agent. "She's got looks, personality, and [obstacles] that she will have had to overcome. She has gone from a co-favorite to an underdog Cinderella, which will triple her appeal."

Nancy's agent, Jerry Solomon, agreed. But he felt that Nancy's main appeal would come from the fact that "she is a real person. When parents bring their kids to skating, Nancy is someone they can relate to. She's not from a wealthy family. She doesn't have a big ego. She's not the most incredible athlete that ever lived, but she warms up to the crowd. People say, 'I can touch and feel that, I can relate to it.' "

Though the Kerrigan family is very proud of everything Nancy has done in her skating career, the medals she wins have never been something any of them—especially Nancy—likes to boast about.

"Our house is so normal," says Mrs. Kerrigan. "In the

whole downstairs there is one picture of Nancy, and there are no medals. There's nothing that makes anybody think skating. It's just not here. It's almost like we're hiding it, and we're not. It's just that this house doesn't tell a story."

As Mary Scotvold once said, "Nancy doesn't even talk about skating when she gets home."

"Somebody asked Nancy, 'Where are your medals?' " Nancy's mother recalls. "Nancy answered, 'Oh, they're shoved in a box.' The person asked, 'Where's the box?' Nancy said, 'Oh, it's shoved in a drawer.' The person couldn't understand why she didn't put the medals out on display. 'What for?' Nancy wondered. 'That's all done, that's over.' "

"Medals tarnish so easily unless you polish them every day," Nancy explains, "so I just put them away."

Even the Olympic bronze medal she won in 1992 is kept in a safe-deposit box, instead of being on proud display. "It's hard on the outside," Nancy said of the medal, "but on the inside, it's crystal and it could just break to pieces if you're not careful. My godson went to pick it up one day and everyone went running to stop him. We figured there had to be a better place for it. For now, the bank. It's safe."

After Nancy won the national championship, some people remarked that she didn't seem too excited about it. "Oh no, I'm very happy," she would say. "I'm pleased, and I love this gold medal, and I'm very glad to be a champion."

She explained that when she was young and started to compete in local tournaments, one of her first coaches warned her that it isn't good to cry when you don't do well and that it isn't good to jump up and down with excitement when you do well. "Otherwise it seems like you're bragging," the coach told her. And bragging, Nancy decided early, was something she never wanted to do.

What Nancy did want to do, does want to do, and *always* will want to do, is to work the hardest she can at whatever she does. And if she does that, she knows one more thing: The people who are the most important to her—her family, her friends, her fans, and herself—will be proud of her no matter how well she does.

Skating Terms

AXEL: the only jump made as the skater moves forward. In a single Axel move, a skater jumps off one foot, turns one and a half times in the air, and lands on the back outside edge of the opposite foot, skating backward. The jump is named for Axel Paulsen, who introduced it in the early 1900's.

CAMEL SPIN: a spin in the spiral position, with one leg extended backward. The arms are often outstretched. A flying camel is a jump from one foot onto the other foot and then into the camel spin.

CHOREOGRAPHY: the arrangement of required jumps, spins, and other skating moves to music of the skater's choice for programs in figure skating and ice dancing competitions.

COMPULSORY FIGURES (also called the school figures or figures): the set patterns upon which figure skating is based; a group of 41 patterns that derive from the two-circle "figure eight" move. In past competitions, skaters had to carve selected figures into the ice with their skates a set number of times, after which judges inspected the resulting marks on the ice for the figure's precision and awarded a score. This is counted for one-third of a singles skater's score. After the 1989–1990 season, compulsory figures were eliminated from the singles competition.

CROSS-FOOT SPIN: a move in which the skater crosses one leg over the other while spinning.

EDGE: either the inside or outside portion of the skate blade.

FIGURE SKATES: Figure skates have two distinct edges on their blades. The two edges—along with the gentle curve of the blade from front to back—make figure skates ideal for skating circles, because the skater can lean on either edge. Figure skates also have a toe pick (see **Toe Pick**), which aids in performing jumps and spins. Hockey skates have only one edge on their blades and no toe pick.

FLIP JUMP: a simple jump in which the skater skates backward, takes off from one foot, makes a full turn in the air, and lands on the opposite foot.

FREE SKATING (also called the freestyle or long program): the part of the competition in which each skater performs a choreographed routine of his or her choosing, usually including a series of jumps, spins, and other moves to music. Two sets of scores are given for free skating; one set is for technical merit, the other is for artistic impression. The free skating program now counts for two thirds of a skater's total score. For women, this program is four minutes long. For the men, it is four and one half minutes long.

GRAND SLAM: refers to a skater or skating couple winning all the major competitions in a single skating season. In an Olympic year, a Grand Slam would include the national championships, the world championships, and the Olympics.

JUDGE: an official who evaluates the performance of each skater or skating pair.

LAYBACK SPIN: a spin performed on one foot. During the spin, the skater arches the back and drops the head and shoulders backward.

LUTZ: a difficult jump in which the skater begins by skating backward on a curve and lands on the opposite foot, jumps and makes a full turn in the opposite direction of the original curve. Named after Alois Lutz, who first completed the jump in Vienna in 1918.

SHORT PROGRAM (also known as the original program): a two-minute-and-forty-second program during which singles skaters execute eight required freestyle moves—such as a double Axel jump or a flying sit spin—to music of each skater's choice. Skaters are given two sets of scores for the short program; one for required elements and one for artistic impression. The short program counts for one third of a skater's total score.

PRESENTATION (also known as artistic impression): is the way a skater moves to the music and the style in which the program is skated. The best skaters don't just skate from jump to jump; they choreograph their program with moves that complement the music.

SALCHOW: a basic jump in which the skater, moving backward, jumps off one foot, makes a full turn in the air, and lands on the other foot. It was first done by Ulrich Salchow, who won the first men's figure skating gold medal, at the 1908 Olympics in London.

SIT SPIN: a spin in a squatting position, on one skate, usually with the free leg stretched out in front of the body. A flying sit spin starts with a jump.

SPIRAL: a skating position taken from ballet, in which one leg is extended up and backward.

SPLIT JUMP: a jump during which the skater kicks his or her legs up and out to each side as if to do a split in the air.

SPREAD EAGLE: a two-foot glide in which both feet are on the same edge of the skate blade, either inside or outside, with the heels facing each other and the toes pointing out.

TOE LOOP JUMP: a simple jump often used in between more difficult jumps or spins. The skater glides backward and begins by using the toe of one foot to push off the ice to help gain height, then revolves once in the air, and lands on the other foot, gliding backward.

TOE PICK: the teeth at the front of the skate blade.

TWO-FOOTED SPIN: a beginner's spin, done with both blades on the ice.

ABOUT THE AUTHOR

Mikki Morrissette is a freelance writer, editor, and genealogist. A genealogist is someone who traces people or families back to their earliest ancestors.

Mikki is a contributing writer to *Sports Illustrated For Kids* magazine. She grew up in Minnesota, which has plenty of ice in the winter, and regrets that she never mastered the art of standing upright on skate blades.

Mikki now lives in New York City, New York.

Silver Blades

by Melissa Lowell

Join the exciting world of figure skating as four
girls try to make their Olympic dreams come true!